Kat + the children
their names but
spelling. Having constantly
changing carers in ones' home
there isn't anywhere I can call
MINE.
I truly hope spelling is being
taught again. To me it's a big
let down when someone are
appreciates in documentaries
or reading the news can
only reach about 7yrs age in
my time. — I'm old-fashioned
I guess and a dunce at
computers & there's the rub.
5 yrs. age are taught. I don't
know where to start.
I recognise the complete
kindness I receive from all
the family. How lucky are we?
I found a good killer. Hilary + Flashy.
Miow. Miow!!.

GLIDING THRO' TIME

Welcome to 'Gliding Thro Time', a collection of my poetry from the last ninety years, starting in 1928.

I invite you to journey with me. I hope you find the poems an inspiring, enlightening peep into social history.

Yes! We all loved Churchill. He kept up our morale through the dark days – come what may! Clustering around the radio, awaiting speeches and that magnificent voice, the jackboots faded away into oblivion.

This is the story of life and love, and the world around us.

Hilary Jill Robson

DEDICATION

To MET

LM

O.G. + C.G
Who gave me encouragement and support

Gliding Thro' Time
© Hilary Jill Robson 2019

Edited by Lisa Marks

WRITING A POEM

Writing a poem is therapeutic
Magnetic between pen, paper and me,
Words expressive and rhythm harmonic.

Prose or verse, adagio, symphonic,
Titled to arouse curiosity,
Writing a poem is therapeutic.

One word, fleet scene may be embryonic
Inspiring description or fantasy,
Words expressive and rhythm harmonic.

Themes profound, light, comedic, prophetic,
Classics surviving to posterity,
Writing a poem is therapeutic.

Strangers' minds meet perhaps empathetic,
Feelings aroused or still tranquility,
Words expressive and rhythm harmonic.

Creating a sojourn charismatic,
Captivating readers to poetry.
Writing a poem is therapeutic
Words expressive and rhythm harmonic.

CAMEO OF MATRON'S MANDATE

Doctor quizzed mother,
We were whizzed away,
Scarlet fever our plague that day.
'Hospital visiting?
Two hours daily!'
Retorted stern-faced matron, facing Mum squarely.
Adding, 'More, causes disorder,
Unless your child dying; on 'Open order'!'
We sobbed when Mother left,
Middle sister's quiet bereft.
Two days later,
'Mother! We're moving her to another hospital 'til dismissal'
'But she likes to feel she's near her sisters,
She's four; to her that will be abysmal!'
Mum's views didn't count, matron's mandate paramount.
'You'll see her by peering thro' glass,
She must not see you, six weeks will soon pass!
Mum protested. 'Two here, one over there,
That will be a thorough nightmare! Neither can I afford the fare
Tight-lipped matron marched elsewhere, she was general in thi
warfare.

Some days we were on our own
While Mum walked to and from sister Joan.
Dad worked shifts, he was riven
Because to him no quarter given.
Young sister and I in different wards
Against system to meet, cause discord.
I was picking skin from flaking lips, resulting in censorship,
Immediately my arms placed into splints;
This cameo impressed indelible imprints
When a matron was king of kings everyone else underlings.

IN THE THIRTIES!

'Dad finishes early today!
We'll have lunch, then on our way!'
'Ooh Mum! Are we going out?' we asked with glee.
'Yes! On a bus to Gran's for tea!'
'Yippee!' A big event to go out!
Bigger and better to be given 'blow-out'!
Cakes, celery, cucumber, new bread, cream, trifle and jellies red,
Arranged on white starched tablecloth, willow-patterned plates outspread.
Gran's feast! We were washed and dressed in Sunday best,
Three excited girls under six years, to be guests.
'Now girls, it's my turn to get ready. I want no antics!
Keep yourselves and frocks spotless. Do nothing hectic!'
Dutifully, we sat side by side on settee,
One read, another sewed and youngest slipped off to wee!
Mum and Dad returned to room, looked around, prepared to go.
'But where's Diane?' they asked, 'Is she playing peek-a-boo?'
We both shook our heads, said, 'Dunno!' Called her name again and again,
But no response ever came.
Searched down and upstairs,
Peered in cupboards, behind chairs,
Then Mum tugged out settee, Diane sat squashed at back, red-eyed and quietly crying.
'You naughty girl! What have you done?
Grab a towel for me quickly, please someone!'
Diane had found a bottle, removed the lid,
Upside down over her spilled contents slid,
Blonde hair to tail she was blotched in ink.
'No time to light copper, child! In you go! Into the sink!
Your new dress is ruined, you'll have to wear old!
What will Gran say about you when she is told?'
Gran who reared six, smiled rumly and fondly, took Diane's head in hand hold.

CHEERFUL DAYS!

Happier the way we were, no discontent
Providing we could pay the rent,
Loaned a 'bob' 'til end of week
To neighbours whose further meals looked bleak.

Friday pay days; Thursday's dinner ever egg,
Boiled, served with soldier's bread,
The treat of steak or chop next day,
Good food expense, good health mainstay.

Neighbours helped each other, payment never sought,
Labour given, none looked for aught,
But would be returned someday
When two pairs of hands needed some way.

Everyone smiled, roundsmen tunefully whistled,
Usual, no-one bristled,
A camaraderie was taught,
Support each other and dread nought.

Children played in street, when a race was begun,
At line-up mothers joined in fun.
Nights, yarns of parents when young,
Worse times, good firm friends they lived among.

Contented, cheerful although short of money,
Small treats made world sunny,
Picnics, bus rides, cakes a delight,
Learned economics overnight.

Our time's blessings, tap dancing, jazz band swingers,
Coppers for baths and laundry wringers!
False 'choppers', tombstone humdingers,
Films, love tales, Westerns, gang gunslingers.

I REMEMBER AIR RAIDS IN LONDON BLITZ

Sirens wailing full blast every night,
Rushing down into Anderson by dimmed torchlight.
Comfortless, on slated bunks 'til sound of all clear,
While single bombs whistled, groups whooshed causing fear,
Thro' experience could gauge where one may explode,
Bunch of bombs falling vicious grapevine overload.

Outside the shelter, searching, spanning,
Floodlighting Luftwaffe trespassing our shut-eye,
Ack-ack volleys firing from nearby battery,
Hun pilots high, out of range, for sanctuary,
Heading for targets, if attacked bombed anywhere,
Limping back to base in Europe for fast repair.

Sometimes, before raids heard RAF overhead,
Gathered to shout good luck in Germany's hotbed,
The Earth trembled from our squadron's moaning low drone,
Heavily bomb-pregnant flew with constant groan,
On return, if clear sky tried to count our boys home,
If one missing screamed delight to spot last home, roam.

Roughly knew the time when foe would take flight
Luftwaffe departed our skies before dawn's light,
Thankfully, the all-clear would cheerfully sound,
We clambered from musty shelter indoor bound,
Jumped into freezing beds for remainder of kip,
Alive but aware others were dead from Hun's blitz.

We kept chickens who squawked all raid in fright,
Fewer precious eggs to collect after bad night,
But staunchly two ducks did not miss their large gifts laid,
Daily awaiting us despite daunting raid.
Relied upon them to conserve our small rations,
Beloved; admired their grit and resolute passion.

IN MIDST OF AN AIR RAID

Midnight round-table debate,
put last ditch case before Father
we daughters would rather
cancel our evacuation departure in morn.
If home should receive a direct hit deathblow
we preferred to have a family tableau
of dying together; not that we kids be left alone.
Dad didn't reply.

Instead eyes skyward, forefinger raised.
'Shush! Listen!' Mum said, Doodlebug overhead.
The monotonous hum drew nearer droned clearer,
we listened intently knowing the score
if ear-marked for us we stood at death's door.
Abruptly the engine cut! A menacing phut!
In ominous moments before missile hit ground
parents sped into action, life-saving bound,
Mum raced upstairs to retrieve sisters from bed,
Dad fled into garden to seek course of warhead.
Too late! Nose-diving whistle! Boom! Instantly know our fate!
House feverishly shuddered, turbulence from blast,
wood and brick debris, shattered glass
whirled around in vortex, then fitfully broadcast.
Bang! Whoosh! The gas main under road ignited,
immense flare-up whole neighbourhood lighted,
pitted with glass I trod over rubble and dirt
fearfully called out to parents, whether alive and unhurt?
Both OK! Heard sisters yelling 'Help! Help!' for aid.
Ceiling fell upon them in slithering cascade.
Draped throughout wreckage of our half destroyed cottage
once heaped clothes for evacuation luggage.

EMIGRATING!

Anxious about
Going to live in a strange land,
Foreign to us and pals, beforehand,
Learned about region second-hand
From others, to make us understand.

We were to live
With foster-folk, old, maybe young,
Another country, somewhere far-flung
And natives spoke in lilting tongue
Where English dwelt too, to be among.

'Live with natives!'
Who wear grass skirts? - 'Not that native!'
We're feeling pensive, apprehensive,
Parents being so persuasive
We three sat sullen and pervasive.

Prior had not
Strayed from home or neck of the woods,
Had lived in our house from babyhood.
Now into junior girlhood
Compelled to leave friends and neighbourhood.

We felt unwell,
Butterfly tummies and shaky,
Too sick to go, hot, headachy,
'You needn't start that *malarkey*
What I say goes in this monarchy!'

On arrival,
Tumbled from carriages like mail,
Saw the natives and turned deathly pale,
Miners blackened head to toenails,
Evacuation to foreign parts – Wales.

AS HE A FARMER WHO STARTED THIS DRAMA?

London evacuees ambling,
Strolling Welsh mountain a'rambling,
We three and visitors mother and aunt,
The latter certainly did not us enchant.

Dressed like an old maid on parade,
Cuban heels, atilt hat, handbag, gloves and all that,
When we espied georgette scarf,
Smothered mouths to stifle a laugh!

We came upon a large walnut tree
No-one owned, full of ripe nuts to our glee.
'Lift me up to shake laden big branch!'
Nuts descended, a hurtling avalanche.

'A man's coming shaking a cane!
Surely he must be a crackbrain!
I bid you farewell, I'm feeling unwell!'
Aunt took off giving loud nervous yell!

We stared as he started to cuss,
Making a beeline directly to us,
Dropping nuts we ran for our lives
Jumping rabbit holes avoiding nosedives.

We had never been runners this day we were stunners,
Steepness gave impetus faster and faster.
More rapid than words from sport's broadcaster.
To our utter amazement a human ball did pass
Aunt rolling over and over in the wet grass.
Landing down-turned on her face,
Topping that, you've guessed, not a hair out of place.

REGIMENT, RANK AND NUMBER

In foreign lands far away
Millions like in deep slumber
Men and boys names starkly etched
Regiment, rank and number,
Impeccable shingle graves,
Countless, white blood-drained crosses,
Frost-white as a winter's dawn,
Marking grim battle losses;
Sudden blood-stained death of sons,
Footprints too young to leave tread,
Men's families cut adrift
No more their lineage bred:
Few words, yet opens black void.
'Died from wounds', 'instantly killed',
Notifications arrive,
War Office mail leaves hearts chilled,
In personal lives and loves;
Camaraderie held dear,
Some won medals, those bereft,
Would prefer them reappear
Than bravery badge in case.
War no longer encumbers
These heroes who gave their lives,
Regiment, rank and number
Must never be forgotten,
Teach history, all aware
Lives given for their freedom,
Remembered, revered in prayer,
Some men teenage, some men sage

REMEMBER

We weep for all the men who gave their lives,
Remember families deprived
Of seeing sons or brothers mature
Because their deaths were premature,
Fathers who did not see first or last child,
Nor the sparkling eyes when baby smiled
They sleep under white crosses in war graves,
Have we proved worthy of peace they gave?

From all continents came keen volunteers,
Those conscripted left in good cheer,
Beforehand some had not strayed village,
Soon embarked troopship, hush-hush voyage,
All battlegrounds fought by three armed forces,
To keep world free with merged resources,
They sleep under white crosses in war graves,
Have we proved worthy of peace they gave?

Do you think of life for them at eighteen?
To see death, injuries obscene,
No life! Camaraderies sustained,
Eased horror and getting crackbrained.
Red poppies are men, some suffered torture,
Youngsters became men without future,
They sleep under white crosses in war graves,
Have we proved worthy of peace they gave?

Mothers and wives received telegrams;
The dreaded paper said 'We regret Ma'am...'
Millions of planted white crosses.
World over, each died a violent death for us.

WITH ONE VOICE

Together we should unite
With one voice,
Tolerate all faiths,
Accept each
And every man's belief.
Give happiness
To those who surround,
Wipe away tears
Of those who are sad,
Or cruelly treated by the bad.
Help us support
Those who are sick,
Mentally, physically;
Ease the pain,
Which, sometimes,
They find hard to explain.
Grant us compassion
To treat the world kindly,
Not bring to bear
Exploitation,
Recklessly blindly.
That will be the day,
Hour and minute,
When we have achieved
The absolute limit,
For us to rejoice
With one voice.

WE STOW OUR BONHOMIE

The spirit of Christmas is loving
And laughter,
Remember to toast
Loved ones in hereafter.

Radiating a warmth to strangers
Who clasp hold
Returning friendly smile
Generously, twofold.

But after festivities, goodwill,
Kind good cheer,
We stow our bonhomie
With tree lights 'til next year.

Why not continue; help someone's day?
Douse looks glum
From those lonely, depressed,
Lift hearts from the humdrum.

Cordiality is infectious,
Pass it on,
Something worthwhile spreading,
Friction, wars would be gone.

LOVING SISTERS' TOGETHERNESS

Four years between three sisters; we are close,
When we're together chatter is jocose,
Times separated, keep in touch by phone,
Dearly love each other, not voiced but shown,
Went about together; wartime children,
In blitz frightened of being left orphans.

Bombed out, survived, a few minor injuries,
Just new 'teens' flustered by our fripperies;
'Bras' and briefs hanging, strung from window frame
Remains, house front lit by gas main aflame;
Than demolished home, left without abode,
Age when undies, sex, subjects sealed, vetoed.

Saturday nights danced, live band, 'til midnight,
Walked home, no transport, arrived at dawn light,
If heard chatting to boys we met, outside,
'Late!' called parents, 'Say goodnight, then inside!'
Morn, Mum sat on bed discussed dance 'til noon
Who were there? Old and new? Any harpooned?
Joyful, together, happy and single,
'No sex girls!' Vowed! Impressed mental jingle.

War ended, division, weddings, children,
'Sister' dates consumed to oblivion,
Some counties between our residences,
Agreed, aged parents must taken precedence.

Helped one sister thro' two family deaths
It's her time now to renew life, draw breath,
Broods have flown nests, sisters three, meet sometimes,
Chat, laughter rings again as in past times,
Year vanish to our springtime, new peacetime,
Regain youth pre-launch of life's pantomime.

OUR LOVELY MUM

Many moons since you slipped away,
Still silently weep every day,
Often long to turn back tideway.

In our mannerisms you stray,
Living on in speech and display,
Many moons since you slipped away.

Yearn to share with you a heyday,
To receive solace on mayday,
Often long to turn back tideway.

When in doubt muse what you would say
Or do it to keep trouble at bay,
Many moons since you slipped away.

All is calm then flares in flambé
When void you left comes into play,
Often long to turn back tideway.

Life is enacting own screenplay,
Coping with roles that fell our way,
Many moons since you slipped away,
Often long to turn back tideway.

MY DEAR DAD

Although you're out of this world and into the next,
If I could pay you a tribute, this would be my text.

You are and always will be my unseen escort,
Your wisdom I use daily, so learned but self-taught,
Fine, common sense enfolds me as home-spun enriching cloak,
Word-painter of life for kin to use and share with other folk.

Look up and never look down,
Or furrow brow into a frown,
Question! Frowning is utter turn down,
Watch, heed, to achieve life's black gown.

Do not join the spilled milk ilk,
Confront your problems, never bilk,
Life can be remains as buttermilk,
Or smooth the curd to feel like silk.

Eyes front and never look back,
Blitzing yourself with needless flak,
Leastways, causing detour or side-track,
Else becoming insomniac.

Without flexibility,
To adapting ability
You will miss an opportunity
If you inject immunity.

Victors stride uphill, onward,
Far-reaching, far-sighted, forward,
Take direct route, journey straight forward,
Waverers roam wayward homeward.

Remember! If coming first doesn't manifest,
You'll be a winner if you've tried your best,
Not the end of the world, a preparatory test
To do our utmost for good while here as God's guest.

MISS YOU OUR PARENTS

We miss you because you cannot see
The closeness of the spread family
Interlaced as plashing,
Living by and passing on your teaching.

Taught optimism not pessimism
Latter leaves one lonesome,
Hope ascends as thistledown
Smoothing the furrows of deep frown.
Learned early, table manners, politeness,
And when shown a kindness,
Remember not to waver
If someone asks to return a favour.

Coached; believe in our own ability,
Reliability,
Never lie just tell the truth
Come what may never be uncouth.
Do not break a pledge nor idly gossip,
Nor offer limp hand grip,
Causes loss of confidence
As does offer through indolence.

Life balances with ill fortune and boon,
Equilibrium's boom,
Economise in hardship,
Be loyal in both love and friendship.
Keep faith with God, do not kow-tow, nid-nod
To would-be demigod,
The choice is blessed happiness
Or a dreary gloominess.
Or later rue the lawlessness.

THE BUTTERFLY

Six feet four tall, athletic, blue eyed,
Hair blond and shoulders wide,
A handsome face and winning smile,
And of dress a certain suave style.

Held ladies all ages in his palm,
Each vying for his charm,
Easy to laugh and quick to please,
In his company all at ease.

He'd raise them in his muscular arms
Twirl around without qualms
Above his head, the young and old,
Giving a high kick, pure gold.

He danced as an uncoiling tight spring,
His splits made mens' eyes sting,
Sang, pleasant Sinatra-style,
He could act too, so versatile.

He filled a room with magnetic presence,
Joy his essential essence,
Men watched filled with envy and awe,
Yearning to attract half his score.

If a girl became too serious,
He'd act imperious,
When that occurred he'd not tarry,
No intention to ever marry.

Not ready to settle and commit,
Preferred a moonlight flit,
Flew away like a butterfly,
No backward glance, thought, turn or sigh.

Ladies returned to down-to-earth men,
Actors best among brethren,
But he'd brought a breath of fresh air,

Made other men exhibit more flair.

TEMPTATION

Temptation surrounds whatever one's age,
Across a room eyes offer invitation
For dazzling flirtatious assignation,
Pressure increasing, hypnotising to engage,
She flattered, flicks lashes to disengage,
Glances again drawn by gravitation,
His dynamic look fires imagination,
Urging her open new romantic page.

She pauses, her marriage has survived dull years,
Gambling would risk losing her loyal loved one,
A dalliance will only end in tears
And a guilt handicap never outrun,
Let ladykiller pass, he will disappear
To green field pastures for sporting fun.

KISMET

Until the day we met
Thought I knew true love
A fantasy.

The moment our eyes met
I knew what true love meant
Dawn thro' sunset.

You are my stars and sky
Far away or nigh
My true Kismet.

RICHES

Love is pairing and sharing, wearing child-bearing,
Smiling and grinning while losing or winning,
Love is flurry and scurry, or calming great worry
Of money, not funny, but grafting brings honey.
Love is caring or swearing, flaring rage blaring,
Rowing and hissing, to bear-hugging, kissing.
Love is fun and exciting, kids biting, in-fighting,
Then war starts to thaw lulled to order of law.
Love is teenagers stinking of bravado drinking,
They do not tarry, move out, maybe marry.
Love is a quietness unknown, when at last we're alone.
Rich freedom about, eat in or dine out?
But:
Love's silence is broken by grandchild awoken,
The kids have not flown, they keep bouncing back home.
Love is ageless and priceless, life toothless and fruitless,
Without life's best date with the world's greatest mate.

PENNING OF LOVE LEAVES

We met when our lives were budding
Love burst into flower
One bloom blossomed into colourful shower
A penning of leaves began.

Brilliant radiance of our love warms
In winter snow,
Brightens long, dark days
And nights giving
Aura candleglow.

Depth of our tender love
Immeasurable in fathoms,
Deep-rooted in bottomless sea,
Surviving all weathers
Calm and stormy.

Constancy of our loyal love
Steadfast as a bedrock,
Or migrating birds
Annually flying
Undeterred to join tropical sunbirds.

As time passes,
Love does not fade
Matures and ripens with age
To another time
And turn of the page.

Book of a dream
A love fantasy
That wonderfully came true
On the wondrous day
You and I met
And I fell in love with you.

JUST ANOTHER DAY

Just another day,
Getting the breakfast
Preparing for work
Quick peck on the cheek
You walked into the murk
Did I look at you? Even reply?
Maybe I gave you an intolerant 'too busy' sigh.
I loved you so much
When did I last say?
If only I'd known
You were to be snatched away!
Soon there would be chaos, complete bedlam
Our unity severed and cosy duo sanctum.
Why you? Why us?
What did we do?
This something outrageous
So disadvantageous!
It was not just another day!

Darling! Quieten! Quieten!
I know you loved me
We'll still be together, I have the pass key
In spirit beside you wherever you go
All the while you need me, I'll be your shadow.
Talk to me! Ask questions silently or aloud
Keep your life running not existing under a cloud,
Were positions reversed and it was I who survived
I know you would want my life to revive!
If you're in a quandary, pray for His help
He understands why sometimes you stand and yelp,

NO ONE KNOWS A WOMAN'S WORTH

No one knows a woman's worth
Until she is not there,
But one misses a woman's mirth
When small things grow to despair.

Who helps to find homework books
Left somewhere known not where?
Does Dad get up to search and look?
What! Get out from snug armchair?

Mum goes visiting parents
Dad stays with meal to heat,
Reads package for a few moments
Still, forgot to pierce clear sheet.

'Mum's home!' kids shout, open door
Kisses, cuddles all around
'Something to eat Mum,' they implore
Micro blew up, baked beans, Dad found!'

Who does washing and cleaning?
Woman of course, who else?
Goes to work and does gardening
But are thanks mumbled heartfelt?

'My clean blouse for tomorrow
Please?' says one. 'And his football kit!'
'Have you looked on the beds? Pronto!
And my shirt,' asks chief culprit?

Is she much loved do you think?
Of course and by the ton,
Woman of worth's family link,
She is their personal sun.

AN ORDINARY DAY IS WONDERFUL

An ordinary day is wonderful,
A wonderful day is bliss,
We, unaware ordinary is wonderful
'Til ordinary fades into blue and missed,
Blue descends to blackness
And blackness into dark,
In darkness hopelessness arrives
Accompanied by bleakness to thrive,
If extra light allowed into darkened heart,
Illumination will lighten anew,
A new anything will be good kick-start,
Ordinary becomes extraordinary, too,
For you,
When ordinary day is wonderful.

LINGERING ECHOES

So close yet so far apart,
must forgo
song in my heart
feel up-tempo
a skip in my step,
we return to burrows,
hurried quickstep,
avoiding dark shadows
to blur others lives,
loving mem'ries, a tryst tableau,
moments poetic,
treasured cameos,
romantic meetings,
lingering echoes,
we met too late,
not free we know,
it cannot be,
commitments grow,
I shall always love you.

LIVING THE PAGES

Almost unnoticed her health began to slide
Until a chest infection bombarded her broadside,
Knocked from her feet, frail legs high into air,
Hospital bedded with constant nursing care.
Later transferred to a residential home
Relinquishing abode she owned, never more to roam.
Gone, her bee freedom
Buzzing to and fro her honeycomb
Another head on life's collision met
Once thought a menacing threat.
Far worse the abject fear than the dreaded deed
When comparing pros and cons above all her needs.
She had clothes, photos and knick-knacks
Recollections in many flashbacks.
Often someone footloose stopped to chat
But, she really missed warm affection of her cat.
Friends and relatives called for chinwag
Sometimes, she, eyeing her handbag
Said, 'Treasures from my whole life in there'
Sadness, happiness, cherished moments thru' years
It is so little to show
After eighty-odd birthdays from embryo.
Nevertheless, the more we live in the past
The less we live in the present
From cobwebs thru' the dust of ages
It has been a wonderful experience living the pages.

A LONESOME SWAN

When I lost you all I could do was cry,
We expected our world to stay the same,
Pushed to back of mind, hoped death would not aim,
Still pairing time before we qualify.
No doubt one would sense as demise drew nigh,
When either name's swan-song pinned in frame,
To be sung when dawn breaks, last lullaby,
One wounded, left behind in life's cruel game.

Shocked when you spread your wings and flew away,
Swam miles before accepting you were gone.
But you were peaceful passing thro' gateway,
Perhaps confirming we shall meet anon,
Yet, await you beside as yesterday
Gliding thro' time being a lonesome swan.

SHADOW ON A RAINBOW

You left suddenly in the night,
My heart's full and life's in limbo,
After trauma caused instant flight,
There's a shadow on my rainbow.

Took for granted happy todays
Improve to happier 'morrows,
But our todays were yesterday
Before shadow darkened rainbow.

Thought we were coupled forever,
Deemed doomsday far distance to go,
Surmised sigh prior dissever,
Deep shadow blacked out our rainbow.

Know you will be there to greet me
When I am beckoned to follow,
Then both of us will feel carefree.
'Til shadow clears from our rainbow.

THE OLD FAMILIAR FACES

Most friends are acquaintances
True friendship hard to acquire
They hit bullseye in any emergencies
Give a hand when you're stuck in quagmire,
Appear without any endeavour
It seems, or upsetting their own busy lives,
Assistance comes; no matter wherever,
Without asking relief just arrives.

No need to meet constantly
Altho' time may have elapsed,
At one's side to cushion the blow tenderly
When a pal's life has promptly collapsed,
Continents and oceans mere kerbstones
To cross, with support for greetings event,
Familiar faces are cornerstones
Without them life would be malcontent.

From earth they do not depart,
Like a boomerang return
To those who confine them with love in their heart;
Offspring's mannerisms replay nocturne.
To possess one such friend is healthy
Counting digits on a hand greatly blessed
When reciprocal both become wealthy
Friendship is the lasting success.

HAPPINESS IS NOW!

Happiness is now!
closeness of family and friends,
we take it for granted
today will never end,
lives will stay the same
as a photograph
or picture in a frame.

Contentment causes
mindless irrationality,
completely ignoring
change is normality,
gaining momentum
with hushed swinging sway
of timeless pendulum.

Suddenly whisked away
by God's hands our struts and later mainstay.

Miss all those we've loved,
the warmth of joyful times we shared,
carefree halcyon days
were gradually pared,
by degrees did we slip
into the mantle,
accepting our heirship.

Miss you to confide
excitement relating good news,
or uplifting when blue,
opinion as we choose.
To you we avow
wherever we meet,
Happiness blossoms somehow.
true happiness is now!

BUT YOU ARE GONE

Birds are still singing,
Flowers are blooming,
But you are gone
Leaving me yearning, mourning.

Couples together
Care not a feather
That you are gone,
Snatched from our lifetime tether.

Weekends are severe
Bank holidays fear
Now you are gone
To heavenly hemisphere.

Life's cold and silent,
Each day is dormant,
Since you have gone
I'm left in bewilderment.

Bobbing in rough sea,
Losing buoyancy,
As you are gone.

PALMS TOGETHER

Palms together
Feel a calm overtake,
A strong arm around you
To accept intake,
For wars to cease,
Replace with peace,
Concentrate to feed
People starving and supply seed
To provide in the good years
All they need
Quench their thirst
Bring water to the door,
Encourage folk to clothe the poor,
Help those who are sick
Visit medic,
Aid those who grieve,
Families bereaved,
Relieve the old from fear,
God bless all far and near,
Palms together.

YOU CAN ALWAYS FIND

Wherever you stray,
Whenever you break to stay,
No matter the hour,
Even less the month nor day,
However leaden the burden
On your shoulders lay,
You can always find
A smile or word to be kind.

Regardless of age,
Whatever colour of skin,
You have a clear option
When trouble lowers a chin,
Behave as a gallant captain
Or untaught urchin,
You can always find
Time for actions to be kind.

Bear in mind, somewhere,
Someday, you are in nightmare
Needing a hand to grasp
And no-one is standing there,
But sharing a similar prayer
To one in despair,
You can always find.

LOVE'S ALSO IN PRAYER

Love is strong, a fort
For the family,
Support in stress,
Compassion easing
Distress, buoyant encouragement
Slaying despair.
Love is eternal with care
Succeeding
Through heirs. Love warms a home, draws
Countless friends, dividends.
From just listening and understanding
When a problem suspends,
Gives refuge after crash-landing,
And clasping arm
Stilling alarm.
Offspring learn early to stand on both feet
Conquering
Disappointment
Or personal defeat.
Love's affection
Cannot be bought nor
Borrowed, not tutor-taught
It is earned;
Unselfishness,
Kindness, do not go
Amiss helping anyone to
Find limitless bliss.
Love and faith in God is there
To those who seek, love's
Also in prayer.

GOD BE IN MY GARDEN

God be in my garden,
God be in my life,
God help us aid others
To keep us free from strife.

God be all around us,
'Specially to those who disregard
You and God and Your teachings,
Thinking they be avant-garde.

God be in our actions,
God be in our words,
Moderate the factions
And let the meek be heard.

God open padlocked gate
To minds shut in dark oblivion
Release the world from hate
To a loving Heaven.
Find You in the millennium.

REMEMBER! BUT FOR THE GRACE OF GOD!

Remember those who are homeless
Casualties of life or war,
Seeking shelter in all weathers
Weary and footsore.

Remember children in famine,
Cadaverous babes' faces,
Crying or inert nearing death;
Sagging skin laces.

Remember disaster victims
Also loved ones left to mourn,
Trying to carry on living,
Their children withdrawn.

Remember when you are happy
Enjoying party fun,
Remember those are less blessed,
Scarcely lives begun.

Give a thought to them and money,
Clothes, 'specs', whatever to hand,
To aid others' harrowing plight,
Labour when undermanned.

Cameramen leave suffering scene
And the headlines quickly replace,
But poor wretches still awaiting
Support to embrace.

Remember to pass round the hat
To guests and those in your clan,
People will give willingly
To help fellow-man.

Remember! But for the grace of God!

LIKE A CAT

Like a cat
I want to curl!
Into a ball
And let the world pass by,
Never again care to unfurl,
Just to lie and quietly waul
Underneath my fallen sky
Aping an injured sleeping cat.

Like a cat
When I felt well
I sensed the sun,
Stood, stretched my aching limbs,
Upon your loss try not to dwell,
All too soon the day is done,
One good life, nine lives are slim,
Unlike the adventurous cat.

Like a cat
Have taken heed,
Do what I wish,
Lazing on summer days,
Seeking new friends to fill a need,
A changed pace helps to banish
Any thoughts to hide away,
I am not a cat seeking prey.

MASTER OF HIS REALM

Do you own a cat? Does he do tricks?
Get into mischief, amuse with antics?
Mine does! Pooch! Colouring aping small tiger,
Intelligent feline, no other cat finer,
Lithe, handsome and striking, bounding swiftly along,
Muscular as a panther, for his size and age, strong,
Hunts prey, not to eat but paw – plonk on head,
He wants them to play, not rigid and dead.

In summer months never fails to wake me at dawn,
My head held with paw, combs mane with southpaw! I yawn and
yawn!
He cat-preens me, claws out, sprucing hair down with tongue
When strands caught midst wee teeth, becomes highly-strung!
I let out piercing shriek, 'Stop! Tangled underneath!'
Pull out hair and ignore him but he's staring beneath,
Those amber eyes do not blink, directly bore into mine,
Without smouldering glare, suddenly makes a beeline
To climb up my body till our noses entwine.

How can I resist a cat with such charm?
I know hour is early but he's doing no harm,
Pooch, gently nips my arm waiting to be fed
From dry cat food packet kept beside bed,
Sated, he twists into air, returns to lie sleepy head
In cat bed; leaving me smiling at determined redhead.

I AM BEST THING IN THEIR LIFE! SO I'LL WRITE!

I, precious cat
Poochy, red hepcat
Who is house boss
Find wheedling gains, not a time loss,
I wrap my owners around my paw,
Those I adopted whilst living next door.

I race down hall
With a ping-pong ball,
Charge up fruit tree,
To show excitement, they're with me
Outside, speeding around as greyhound
Corner, leaning over, close to ground.

Plead with my eyes
Nuzzle; 'til questioned 'Why?'
Lead, way to dish
Sit really awaiting fish,
Peer pertly thro' banisters to charm,
Gets them each time, winsome, appealing smarm.

If fed by hand
I feel very grand,
They squat for me,
Offering tidbits, tongue tasty,
I bear in mind to keep lithe figure,
To banish trespassers, need my vigour.

They will agree
Best in world Poochy
They know my game,
But love me dearly, just the same,
I am a bundle of love and fun,
On depressing days, I am rays from sun.

I'M A CLEVER LAUGHING CAT

Know how to be fed at night
With dry food, firstly polite,
Gently prod bare skin in sight,
No luck! Push nails in skin tight,
Wakens, feeds, too tired to fight,
I'm a clever laughing cat.

She thinks I should use my flap,
Growing fatter it's cat trap,
I'm built a well-rounded chap,
With paw tap flap, ignored, zap,
Up she jumps to open gap,
I'm a clever laughing cat.

If I dislike new menu,
Refuse to eat and poo-hoo,
'Eat up Pooch and don't pooh-pooh!'
She says, 'Change of food for you!'
Throw wobbly, it's back on cue,
I'm a clever laughing cat.

When friends call and do not kneel
To stroke me, they come to heel,
When I nudge, nudge them to feel
My soft coat their hearts I steal,
Paws in air, on back appeals,
I'm a clever laughing cat.

Have happy disposition,
No wish for expedition,
Found home on hunting mission,
Chase away competition,
Know my place, top position,
I'm a clever laughing cat.

I AM BEAUTIFUL

I am beautiful,
People travel from afar to look at me,
When sometimes I lay bare they do not sight see,
Loving me for what I am, their chickadee.

I often dress in resplendent radiance,
My main aim being to attract an audience,
A regal sight to behold,
I'm known for wearing masses of gold.

Artists find me irresistible,
Poets enjoyable,
All find me approachable,
Just occasionally impossible, being impassable.

If I am neglected,
I become dejected,
Run wild in disarray,
Looking attractive, at my best, my metier.

Constant attention is my goal, unashamedly,
Many spend their lives with me,
To show appreciation and glee,
I blossom and bloom thro' the year, profusely,
Me boast? I beg your pardon
I am your garden.
I am an exquisite garden.

PURE MAGIC!

As spring just dawning
I, enjoying morning,
Chilly; as sun held no heat,
Heavy dew spawned, airborne;
Sequin spangled lawn,
Of my hidden personal retreat.

Viewing bulbs new blooms,
Hyacinth scented perfume
Permeating garden moist air,
From floral podium
Of season's blossoms,
Opening dance movement premiere.

Gazing at daffodils,
One trumpet, beyond frill,
Sat an inch-long baby frog,
Drinking clear pearls of dew;
While transfixed I grew,
Awoke knowing indoors I must jog.

Grabbed my camera,
To snap adventurer,
Returned, stooped, ready to click,
Wee frog gracefully leapt
Into white cloudlet
Snowdrops; ballet, nature's pure magic.

A stunning moment,
Cameo enchantment,
Colour captured in my mind,
Seeking sequel each spring
Tiny frog vaulting
To photo, captivate and spellbind.

MAN AND TREE

Some trees
Lifespans are similar to man's,
Saplings grow, bear fruit
Produce hardy clan,
Suffer seasonal shake-ups,
Seasons serene,
When robust and rugged,
Part of the scene
As they grow older
Weakness appears,
Looking weather-beaten; strength
Starts to disappear.

Man and tree
Experience gales and
Tornadoes through years,
Ferreting those with feet of clay,
Weak and feeble blown to ground,

Returned again to Mother Nature,
Great statures laid low,
Ashes to ashes, earth to earth,
Man and tree echoed.

UNDERSTANDING TREES

Trees the supreme plants of earth
Without them mankind would have died at birth,
Stout main trunks, slender branches spread,
They grow globally but some men cut them dead;
Do not overlook they live and breathe as you
A circulation system and digestive avenue.

To the earth's and their advantage,
Trees breathe through the underside of leafage
Separating elements of air,
Carbon absorbed;
Oxygen reverted to the atmosphere,
Circulation; from foot hair to furthest leaf
Via sapwood travelling slowly cell to cell without relief.

Wending from small to larger roots,
Meandering trunk, branches and offshoots,
In the leaf into food it's transformed
With the aid of sunlight carbon is reformed,
When blended tree food returns by way of cells
Thro' inner bark homeward to nourish last radicels.

The tree makes this transformation,
In the human race it's called digestion,
Building layer cells as it proceeds,
Trees' raw food brought along in the sap for needs,
Water dearth the roots delve steeper and deeper,
Lacking nourishment forages afield as a minesweeper.

Trees resist animal or bird,
Continue shielding soil from sun, undeterred,
Preserve natural springs of the earth
Preventing land becoming grave of stillbirth,
Humanity cannot exist without trees
Majestic plant nature's master of ceremonies.

Trees do not need mankind, man's mainly the foe.

COTTAGE GARDEN SECRETS

A minute seed, cutting, new shoot
Or maybe a tiny root,
Hand-sown or dropped by a bird
The gift unseen also unheard
Covered with soil by Mother Earth,
She's aptly named, profuse at birth,
However long you stand and stare
When seedlings sprout one's never there,
Secret time between God and the ground,
To thrive and arrive when no one's around.

The stem and leaves daily grow strong
Enlarging before birdsong,
Another peep tight buds seen
Merging amid stems self-same green,
Next sighting a colour's peeking
God's enlightening to those seeking,
Perfect bud to flawless flower,
Bees collecting within hour,
Later, beautiful plant in full bloom
Or succulent fruits and 'veg' to consume.

Bustling insects, small animals,
Cats watching home-run channels
Of hedgehogs and holes of shrews,
Favourite feline rendezvous,
Each sitting at entrance in turn
Day, duty guard, stone-still nocturne,
Learning from Nature's mixed bouquet,
Intricate jigsaws every day,
God's garden, nature, life intertwine
Tightly together as tendrils on vine.

WINTER TAKES FLIGHT

Snowdrops oscillating in the wind
Proclaiming momentous news,
Forsake winter awaken to spring
All vegetation, wildlife,
Birds on the wing.

Northern gales lessening to tepid breeze,
Sun rays fleetingly flicker,
Encouraging new cycle to emerge,
Warming iced slumber for
Growth to resurge.

Winter does not easily succumb
Tries to shackle regained hold,
But spring's tug-of-war team has sun as might
Lingering later daily;
Winter takes flight.

Awaiting a salubrious birth
The expectant life on Earth.
Main reason our sphere continues to spin
Most species renew when spring
Showers in.

Mans' plod changes to positive stride,
Strangers greet with kindling smile,
Long winter heaviness begins to lift
When we glimpse supreme talent
Of nature's gift.

Renewal, freshness kisses mankind,
Thoughts turn to weddings and love
Maybe start again in different employ
Perhaps, just stop to unwind and
Springtime enjoy!

PRELUDE TO SPRING

A treasure hunt at winter's demise
Reveals natures' ingenious surprise,
To those who care to search for the plant;
The one that never fails to enchant,
As it gives seasonal cohesion
Adjoining wintertime to the next season.

Seeking shoots of spear-shaped leaves,
Awesome strength these small plants achieve,
Thrusting thro' frost-bitten soil,
Eagerly awaiting the buds to uncoil.

Pure white, waxen, heavily crowned heads,
Christening the damp, dark, flowerless beds,
Colossal might; hard to envisage
Veiled, skirt-dancing in green foliage,
Pinnacled in white busby-style hat,
Relaying, 'stand-by' message; spring's diplomat.

Withstanding gales, rain, sleet and snow,
Buoyantly swaying to and fro,
Pearl bells; silently ringing,
Arousing spring bulbs while nonchalantly swinging.

Awakening plants some twice their size,
Inspiring them to prepare; mobilise.
These magnificent first-footing flowers
Majestic; yet with heavy-weight powers,
Vying the elements; non-stop,
Continuous ringing from winning snowdrops.
A prelude to spring the intrepid snowdrop.

SUMMER SUN-KISSED DAYS

Summertime, lawn, daisy days,
Winter worries aground,
Summertime, halcyon days,
Happy high jinks abound,
Summertime, long lazy days,
Breezy blossoms rebound,
Holiday love, fast friendship days
In foreign and home playgrounds.

Drifting fragrance, wafting days,
Plentiful fruits astound,
Juice lusciously oozing days,
Picked and popped, tasted renowned,
Barbecue and picnic days,
Mens' cooking to foreground,
Grills, salads and shashlik days,
Entertaining, 'til sundown.

Summer months are sun-kissed days,
Peace loving as a dove,
Summer days are blissful days,
Blessed by the one above.

SEIZE EACH PRECIOUS DAY

Seize each precious day as dawning wakens,
Clasp first fleeting moments of light's first blush,
To leave it virginal and unbroken
Is to delete Venus with an airbrush.

Unused time squandered within life's measure,
Our meted span is set from cry of birth,
Minutes tick away with work or leisure
Do make seconds worthwhile living on earth.

The clock idles when we are world-weary,
Staleness or flatness are monotony,
Climbing a new hill clears eyes too dreary,
Scuttling boredom to sea of destiny.

Heed an underfed leaf withers on tree.
Slowly fading to become absentee.

UNDISCIPLINED DRIVERS

Taxiing to hospital
We are in Agra, not the capital,
Transport cumbersome, dated, unfamiliar,
No traffic code here in India.
Vehicles criss-cross highway, this way and that,
Only stop if they break down or for a tyre-flat,
No-one is trapped in an enmesh,
Nothing interferes with this seething mesh.
Gesticulating drivers, ill-tempered, grumpy,
Roads are churned up, dusty, bumpy,
Several carts ambling, bumbling; oxen-drawn,
Motorists with fingers permanently on the horn.
No traffic lights or rights of way,
But directing this ants nest every day,
Standing on a rostrum, gun and truncheon-armed cop,
White gloved hands signalling, non-stop.
Owners of lorries, trucks, ringing handbells,
Off-side and near-side wings dented, cracked like eggshells,
Cycle rickshaws, cheap runabout,
A policeman stops one, argues, then hand clouts
Several times around the head, know not what about!
Foreign passengers expressing doubt,
Apparently wishing they could get out.
Only the sacred cow is shown great love and care,
Detouring her on the thoroughfare,
Allowed to roam and wander aimlessly,
To do as she wishes quite unreservedly.
Pinch myself! Am I in a talkie?

IN THE LAND OF THE TIGER

City condensed, swathed by shroud
Smothering, hazy pollution cloud,
Friend became breathless, persevered
Breathing laboured, often sheared,
She slogged wearily from little exertion
On guided Indian day-excursion,
Respiration worsened, not just atmosphere,
Condition life-threatening my ominous fear,
Lagging, severed from lumbering crocodile
She, hardly moving, nigh immobile.
Bystanders hardened to illness, inure,
Our absence unnoticed by rest of the tour,
Beggars encircled us being lone prey,
Pauper – becalmed felt alarmed by foray.
As countless hands thrust from every direction,
Tempted to shove for air; spread arms for protection,
Into our faces puny babies were plunged
When opportunists rapaciously lunged,
Urchins, cripples, ancients and poor,
Untimely cadging we were forced to ignore,
Trapped, in need of urgent salvation,
Medical aid, freed from intimidation.
Reassured pal; left with qualms made a dash,
To the Red Fort located guide in a flash,
Upon return found impoverished dispersed,
Another tourist coach-load beggar immersed,
Summoned rickshaw ridden by vagabond
Asked again for payment when we reached back of beyond.
Eventually friend received hospitalization.

THE SUN BLINKED

Dewdrops on roses are my tears,
Your spirit left; I am alone,
The sun blinked mid our dazzling years.

Severed; But complete I appear,
Showing breeze not force of cyclone,
Dewdrops on roses are my tears.

You closed your eyes to disappear,
Out of bounds to heavenly zone,
The sun blinked mid our dazzling years.

Expecting you to reappear,
Mindless when I know you have flown,
Dewdrops on roses are my tears.

Shall mourn and learn to persevere,
Chipping away heartbreak milestone,
The sun blinked mid our dazzling years.

Survivors climb mountain 'til clear
Of debris from loss of keystone,
Dewdrops on roses are my tears.

ALONE!

Not just yesterday
But today
And all the tomorrows,
I miss and need you,
Perpetually yearning,
A constant pain of aching sorrow;
Crave another sight, another word,
Since you were unexpectedly called,
When the death-knell boomed
The very heart of our lives stalled,
Then ceased to exist;
Doomed,
Leaving me alone;
Gone temporarily both closeness and nearness,
Our being together postponed,
Until a time, date unknown,
We resume in familiar harness.

We realise death knocks at every door,
But fail to recognise the submerging void,
Stark isolation in a bog on a dark, desolate moor.

AGES OF RHYME

From babyhood we are sung tales,
Hushed lyrical lullabies rarely fail,
Tuneful nursery rhymes, 'Baa! Baa! Black Sheep,'
Relax tots alertness before nights sleep,
Taught to memorise from three-letter words,
Later, some which were previously unheard,
Repeating as a mynah bird.

Kindergarten rhymes are showpiece
For infants to recite as party-piece,
Remembering other nursery rhymes,
Showing-off to parents prior bedtimes,
Receive Christmas and birthday cards in verse,
See 'Pantos' some couplets to converse,
Easy for cast when they rehearse.

Ballad lyrics, also 'Pop' songs,
Hymn words and anthems flow, lilting along
To rhythmic stanzas heard all thro' the day,
Multiplication tables learned times way,
Slogans, advertisements, jingle refrains,
So catchy the music lodges in brain,
Simple to recall or retain.

No one can obliterate rhyme,
There throughout life until end of our time,
Commenced in dark pages of history,
Many stories preserved in poetry,
Writers enjoy freedom penning in prose
Vie, reasoning rhythmic rhyme to compose,
Fettered yet challenging verse foes
In ages of rhyme.

TINY STAR OF NEW BEGINNINGS

She was born and then...
Later found
She could not hear the loudest sound.
This beautiful tot full of joy,
Bubbly, friendly to girl or boy,
Especially if they were sad,
Weeping doleful tears, she did not hear,
But toddled toward to be near,
Soon making herself understood,
Her new pal no longer wet-eyed,
As the crying had stopped, face dried.

Mummy kept a vigilant eye,
To guard her babe,
Who could not hear her name when called.
To keep her safe most important aim.
A strain, but she at no time palled.
All family learned sign language,
Which added appeal to this mite,
Who was so eager to copy,
Agog to learn, in fact a captivating turn.

At age of two a huge breakthro'
After numerous doctors tests,
A London's children's hospital,
With Amy were really impressed.
Physically sound, mentally poised,
She would gain, succeed with great zest,
From cochlea implant 'op'. She was surely blessed!

Firstly volume kept very low,
Acclimatising her noise flow.

BEDTIME POEMS

Please Lord,
Help others, especially kin,
To think of those living alone,
Left battered and bruised by life's cyclone
Silently, suffering pain within.

FOUR FURTHER REFLECTIONS

No one knows who,
No one knows when,
Someone takes last breath, forever
Endeavour not to rue,
Endeavour not to yen,
Any words or deeds forever.

A stone thrown in pond makes ripples,
A rock thrown makes waves
But each return.

Emit a smile and it will return,
Emit a groan and back comes a moan.

Yesterday is history,
Tomorrow never comes,
Today is reality,
Make it a day to remember.

A LIFE BONUS

True friends are thin on the ground,
May take years before one is found,
Always there in times of trouble,
When life bursts as a soap bubble,
If tears rain face because love strays
Be there too, it works both ways.

Listen while friend pours from heart
Worrying problems to impart,
You may suggest but not to stress
She will learn not to acquiesce
All the time, for full happiness
To another's bossiness.

Good friend is stairway to sky
Escalating your down to high,
Birth, anniversary, dating,
One firm friend for celebrating
Acquaintances not a minus
My friend is my life's bonus.

SONNET OF A LIFE TOGETHER

Wherever I am, wherever I go,
When not together I am not alone,
Foremost in my thoughts, my constant shadow,
We are united as one cornerstone.

Any misfortune faced as a stronghold,
Kissed away teardrops of any sorrow,
Shielded woes unknown, only lately told.
With deft and skilled hand solved by the morrow.

You loved me when young and love me now old,
Say wrinkles add character to my face,
Attract relatives, friends to our threshold,
By relaxed atmosphere, warmth of embrace.

It has always been my life's endeavour
To make you happy as I, forever.